D0480975

MACHINES RULE

IN THE AIR

Steve Parker

W
FRANKLIN WATTS
LONDON • SYDNEY

This edition 2012

First published in 2008
by Franklin Watts

Franklin Watts
338 Euston Road
London NW1 3BH

Franklin Watts Australia
Level 17/207 Kent Street
Sydney, NSW 2000

Editor: Jeremy Smith
Design: Billin Design Solutions
Art director: Jonathan Hair

A CIP catalogue record for this book
is available from the British Library.

ISBN 978 1 4451 0928 2

Printed in China

Picture credits: Agencia Mendoza/Sygma/Corbis: 21br. © Airbus SAS. All rights reserved: 8bl, 8br, 9tr, 9bl, 9br, 16b. Stephan Aufschnalter/epa/Corbis: 12b.Bettmann/Corbis: 26t. © Boeing Company. All rights reserved: 7t, 10t, 10b, 14b, 15bl, 15tr, 18, 19bl, 19br, 22-23c, 28-29, 30. Gary James Calder/Shutterstock: 13tr. Lance Cheung/USAF/Topfoto: 11br. Dan/Shutterstock : 21tl. Dryden Flight Research Center/NASA: 27tl. Joerge Ferrari/epa/Corbis: 4-5, 13b. S. Feval/Le Matin/Sygmas/Corbis: 21bl. James Fraser/Rex Features: 11tr. Timothy E. Goodwin/Shutterstock: 7c. H. Goussé © Airbus SAS. All rights reserved: 8-9. George Hall/Corbis: 16t. Stephen Hind/Reuters/Corbis: 1. Robert Kyllo/Shutterstock : 17b. Langley Research Center/NASA: 27b, 27tr, 27br. David Le Bon/Transtock/Corbis : 17c. © Lockheed Martin Corporation. All rights reserved: front cover t, 2, 3, 6, 14t, 15tl, 15br, 19t, 20, 23t, 23b, 25tl, 26b. Peter MacDiarmid/Rex Features: 25bl. Elizabeth Opalenik/Corbis: 21tr, 31. Rex Features: 11tl. Dibyangshu Sarkar/AFP/Getty Images: 24, 25tr. Skyscan/Corbis: 12t, 13tl. Jim Sugar/Corbis : front cover br, 7b. Todd Taulman/Shutterstock : front cover bl. UNSCOM/Corbis: 22b. US Navy © Boeing Company. All rights reserved: 25br. US Navy/Ensign John Gray © Boeing Company. All rights reserved: 11bl. Robin Utrecht/ANP/epa/Corbis: 17t. Brad Whitsitt/Shutterstock: 17tr.

Franklin Watts is a division of Hachette Children's Books, an Hachette UK company.

www.hachette.co.uk

CONTENTS

Blast off!

The engines roar, the power surges, the wheels rumble and the wings tremble... Up, up and away into the clear sky. Get ready for take-off on an exciting journey through the air.

There are many different types of aircraft. Jet planes take people on holiday all over the world. Helicopters can hover in the air and are used by the army and emergency services. Spy planes and fighter planes protect countries while stunt planes allow pilots to show off their skills!

Military planes

Most countries have an **air force**. Fighter planes can help defeat enemy aircraft while 'invisible' spy planes can spot other aircraft without being seen themselves.

Helicopters

Helicopters can hover in the air. This means they can go almost anywhere. They are used to rescue people in danger and by air forces all over the world.

Jet planes

Many people travel by jet plane when they go on holiday. These planes range from small aircraft to super-**jumbos** that can carry hundreds of people at a time.

Stunt planes

If pilots want to show off their skills for fun, they fly stunt planes. These planes can go upside down, spin around and much more!

Super-jumbo

The biggest planes in the world are super-jumbos. The original jumbo jet was the Boeing 747, which first flew over 30 years ago. The largest, newest super-jumbo is the Airbus A380.

The A380 is a double-decker, with two floors all along the **fuselage**. One version can carry 800 people in standard class. The other seats 520 in first, business and standard class.

The brand new A380 jumbo was launched to a fanfare of music, flashing lights and fountains of water from special airport fire engines.

Stats and Facts

Airbus A380

Maker: Airbud (European)

Length: 73 metres

Wingspan: 79.8 metres

Height: 24.1 metres

Weight empty: 250 tonnes

Weight fully loaded: 590 tonnes

Engines: 4 Rolls Royce Trent 970/977s or EA GP7,200s

Cruising speed: 900 km/h

THAT'S INCREDIBLE

The A380 is unlikely to damage runways because it has 22 wheels, four more than a Boeing 747.

Test pilots first flew the A380 in April 2005.

The jet engine has a massive fan with blades on it.

There is plenty of room to relax in a first class seat!

Fighter-bomber

Missiles

The fighter-bomber is the cutting edge of today's air force. It flies deep into enemy land, stays low to avoid radar, delivers its radar-guided or heat-seeking missiles and laser-guided bombs, then roars back to safety.

The F-15 Eagle is one of the world's best all-weather strike aircraft. The pilot sits in front. The rear seat is for the Weapons Systems Officer, WSO, nicknamed 'wizzo'.

Stats and Facts

F-15E Strike Eagle

Maker: McDonnell Douglas/ Boeing (USA)

Length: 19.4 metres

Wing span: 13 metres

Height: 5.6 metres

Weight empty: 14 tonnes

Weight fully loaded: 36 tonnes

Engines: 2 Pratt & Whitney F100-229s

Top speed: 2,690 km/h

THAT'S INCREDIBLE

The F-15E Eagle can blast straight upwards at the rate of 250 metres every second!

Missiles and bombs (above) are stored under the wings.

As the jet engines boost the fighter-bomber through the **sound barrier**, shock waves form and make a sonic boom that sounds like thunder.

Fighter pilots wear helmets with oxygen masks to help them breathe.

Super stunter

The highlight of any air show is a display by an aerobatic or stunt plane. Loops, rolls and dives thrill the crowd. Then the coloured smoke switches on and the plane makes amazing patterns in the sky.

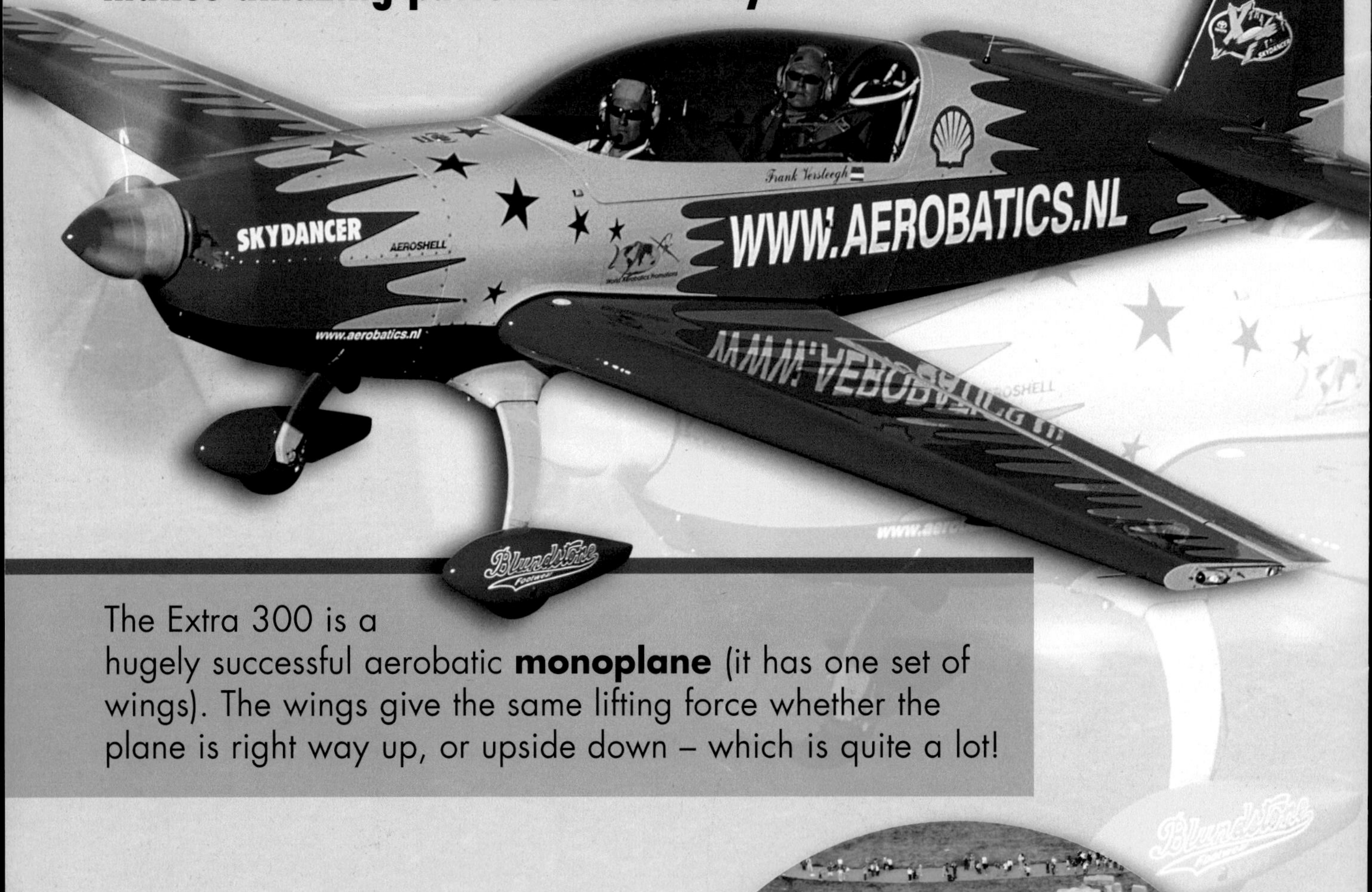

The Extra 300 is a hugely successful aerobatic **monoplane** (it has one set of wings). The wings give the same lifting force whether the plane is right way up, or upside down – which is quite a lot!

Flying in close formation takes great skill.

THAT'S INCREDIBLE

A stunt plane can twirl or spin right around in less than a second.

Stats and Facts

Extra 300

Maker: Extra Flugzeugbau (Germany)

Length: 6.95 metres

Wing span: 7.4 metres

Height: 2.62 metres

Weight empty: 680 kg

Weight fully loaded: 950 kg

Engine: AEIO-540 L1B5

Extra 300 pilots get used to performing incredible stunts. They can spin around and turn upside down, although pilots may be sick at first!

Planes race around a circuit marked out by tall blow-up pylons.

Stealth planes

How can a plane be invisible? Stealth planes are, but only on a radar screen. Radar is used to detect aircraft hundreds of miles away. Stealth technology means these planes don't show up on the enemy's screen.

The F-22 Raptor stealth fighter joined the US Air Force in 2005. The angle of the gas blast from its jet engines can be altered for faster twists and turns, which is called thrust vectoring.

The B-2 Spirit stealth bomber is one of the strangest shapes in the sky.

Radar uses radio waves that bounce back off the aircraft. But the B-2's shape means the radio waves bounce away at all angles and can't be detected.

THAT'S INCREDIBLE

The B-2 Spirit stealth bomber is the world's most costly aeroplane. You'd need more than $2 billion to buy one – if it were allowed.

The F-117 Nighthawk fighter was one of the first stealth planes.

Stats and Facts

B-2 Spirit stealth bomber

Maker: Northrop Grumman (USA)

Length: 20.9 metres

Wing span: 52.1 metres

Height: 5.1 metres

Weight empty: 70 tonnes

Weight fully loaded: 150 tonnes

Engines: 4 General Electric F118-GE-100s

Top speed: 760 km/h

In the air traffic control room, each 'blip' on the screen is an aircraft. But stealth planes produce no blips at all.

Private jet

If you want to go somewhere faraway and fast, in luxury – take the plane! But not a regular passenger flight. You need your own private plane like a Learjet (below) , complete with pilot and co-pilot, and crew who attend to your every need.

THAT'S INCREDIBLE

To hire a private jet usually costs at least £1,000 per hour. That's cheaper than buying one, however. They cost around £5 million!

Inside, the private jet is like a luxury hotel room.

"Welcome aboard!" If it is safe, you can have a chat with the pilot and look at the dials and controls.

A Learjet's tanks hold 70 times more fuel than a family car.

Stats and Facts

Learjet 45XR

Maker: Bombadier (USA)

Length: 17.8 metres

Wing span: 14.6 metres

Height: 4.3 metres

Weight empty: 6.2 tonnes

Weight fully loaded: 9.5 tonnes

Engines: 2 Honeywell TFE71s

Cruising speed: 840 km/h

Private jets aren't always small. This Boeing 747 **Jumbo** is a private jet used by presidents of the United States of America.

Helicopter gunships

Guns

Missiles

Rockets

The AH-64 Apache is one of the world's most fearsome fighting machines. This attack helicopter bristles with guns, rockets and missiles, and it can fly and land almost anywhere.

Stats and Facts

AH-64 Apache

Maker: Hughes/Boeing/ McDonnell Douglas (USA)

Length: 17.7 metres

Rotorspan: 14.6 metres

Height: 3.8 metres

Weight empty: 5.1 tonnes

Weight fully loaded: 9.5 tonnes

Engines: 2 General Electric T700-GE-701s

Cruising speed: 270 km/h

The Apache carries its weapons on the side of the helicopter.

THAT'S INCREDIBLE

The Apache Longbow can fire its missiles accurately even while it is hiding out of sight behind a hill!

Apaches hover low over an airfield, ready to fire their rockets. Luckily this is just a practice to test the equipment.

The pilot's screens show all kinds of information, from height and speed to how much fuel is left.

Balloons & airships

How do balloons and airships fly if they don't have wings? Airships are powered by a gas called *helium*, and have engines and propellers. Balloons are usually round and have no engines. They fly using just hot air.

Gondala

The big part of an airship is filled with helium. The passengers sit in the cabin, or gondola, underneath.

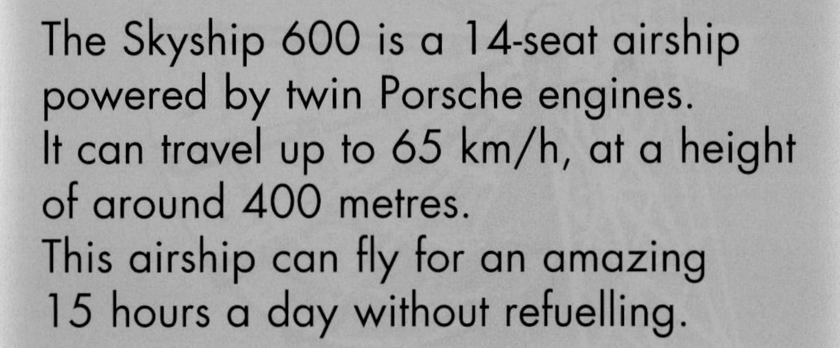

The Skyship 600 is a 14-seat airship powered by twin Porsche engines. It can travel up to 65 km/h, at a height of around 400 metres. This airship can fly for an amazing 15 hours a day without refuelling.

A balloon contains hot air, which is lighter than cold air and floats upwards.

Stats and Facts

Skyship 600

Maker: Global Skyship Industries (USA)

Length: 66 metres

Volume: 7,600 cubic metres

Height: 22 metres

Weight: 5.5 tonnes

Personnel: Pilot, co-pilot, 12 passengers

Engines: 2 Turbo charged Porche 930s or Textron Lycoming 10-540s

Cruising speed: 65 km/h

THAT'S INCREDIBLE

Steve Fossett made more long-distance balloon trips than anyone else. In 2002 he flew solo non-stop around the world by balloon.

Airlifters

Cargo, freight and transport aircraft are known as airlifters. They must be strong, tough and easy to take off and land, because their runways are not always very smooth.

nose

Cargo is loaded onto the Boeing C-17 at the front, through the aeroplane's nose.

The C-5 Galaxy can carry goods weighing the same as 1,700 people, or three battle tanks.

THAT'S INCREDIBLE

Inside, the Galaxy's cargo compartment is half a metre longer than the very first aeroplane flight by the Wright brothers, way back in 1903.

Stats and Facts

C-5 Galaxy

Maker: Lockheed (USA)

Length: 75.3 metres

Wing span: 67.9 metres

Height: 19.8 metres

Weight empty: 170 tonnes

Weight fully loaded: 380 tonnes

Engines: 4 General Electric TF39s

Cruising speed: 900 km/h

The C-130 Hercules is the most successful airlifter. It is used by air forces and by airlines, as a cargo carrier, in more than 50 countries.

Straight up and down

Jump jets are fighter planes that can take off by going straight up, and land by coming straight down. This is called VTOL – Vertical Take-Off and Landing.

Nozzles

The Harrier is the most famous jump jet. Air for the Harrier's jump jet's engine enters the filters on the side of the plane. Four moveable **nozzles** direct the jet blast downwards for take-off and landing, and rearwards for level flight.

THAT'S INCREDIBLE

The Harrier has starred in more films than any other plane, from James Bond's *Living Daylights* to Arnold Schwarzenegger's *True Lies*.

Harriers take off and land anywhere, from a woodland clearing to the swaying deck of an aircraft carrier.

Stats and Facts

Harrier II

Maker: British Aerospace (UK)/Boeing/McDonnell Douglas (USA)

Length: 14.1 metres

Wing span: 9.2 metres

Height: 3.5 metres

Weight empty: 5.7 tonnes

Weight fully loaded: 8.5 tonnes

Engines: Rolls Royce Pegasus 105

Cruising speed: 1,000 km/h

The F-35 Lighting II lands vertically using a large, down-facing fan-propeller.

The V-22 Osprey has engines and propellers at its wing ends. These face up for vertical take-off, then swing around to point forwards for normal flight.

Record breakers

Fastest, highest, longest – the world of aircraft is full of amazing records and feats. Here are some from over the years.

Concorde was the world's only faster-than-sound passenger plane. It could cruise at 2,100 km/h. It first flew in 1969 and retired in 2003.

The SR-71A Blackbird spyplane flew faster and higher than any other civilian or military aircraft. In 1976, it set the world speed record of 3,529 km/h and the height record of 25,929 metres.

THAT'S INCREDIBLE

The longest wings on any aircraft are on the Hughes H-4 "Spruce Goose", a one-off giant seaplane with a 97.54 metres wingspan!

Stats and Facts

X-15

Maker: North American (USA)

Length: 15.45 metres

Wing span: 6.8 metres

Height: 4.12 metres

Weight empty: 6,620 kg

Weight fully loaded: 15,420 kg

Engines: XLR-99 Rocket Engine

Max speed:

7,274 km/h

The X-15 was the USA's last experimental 'X plane'. It was not so much an aircraft, more a rocket with wings and a pilot. It flew at over 7,200 km/h in 1967.

The Bell X-1 rocket plane was the first aircraft to go supersonic – faster than sound, in 1947.

The speediest propeller plane was the Grumman F8F Bearcat, at 850 km/h.

Glossary

Air force
A group of planes a country uses to protect itself against attack.

Airlifter
A very large aircraft that can carry extremely heavy loads.

Fan
In a jet engine, the huge spinning many-bladed part at the front, which works as an intake fan for the engine and as a propeller.

Formation
When aircraft fly near each other, forming an overall pattern such as a V or X.

Fuselage
The main body of an aircraft, which is usually long and tube-shaped.

Helium
A lighter-than-air gas, used in airships and some balloons (also found in some party balloons).

Jumbo jet
A very big aircraft with jet engines, carrying hundreds of passengers, usually on two floor or decks – the Boeing 747 was the first jumbo.

Loop
When a plane goes up and over on its back, upside down, and them comes down to fly level again, tracing a circle in the sky.

Monoplane
Aircraft with one pair of main wings, left and right, rather than a double pair as in a biplane.

Nozzle
A hole or tapering tube, especially on a jet engine, to alter the direction of the jet blast.

Radar
Sending out radio waves to bounce off objects, then detecting the returning echoes to find the direction, distance and size of the object. Radar stands for Radio Detection And Ranging.

Roll
When a plane tilts one wing down and the other up and keeps going, to twist around upside down, then carry on until it is right way up again, all the time flying forwards.

Roll out
When a new plane is first revealed to the public, reporters and cameras, usually by rolling it out of its hangar.

Stealth plane
An aircraft which is difficult to detect in various ways – on a radar screen, from its noise, from the radio signals it sends out, from the heat in its engines and so on.

Sound barrier
When an aircraft flies faster than the speed of sound it 'breaks the sound barrier' and causes a deep thud or sonic boom.

Test pilot
A very skilful pilot who flies the first versions of an aircraft to check it all works well, is safe and flies properly.

VTOL
Vertical Take-Off and Landing. A plan that can take off by going straight up and land by coming straight down.

Find out more

http://www.howstuffworks.com/airplane.htm
Explanations about how all kinds of aircraft and their parts work.

http://www.century-of-flight.net/
Huge site celebrating 100 years of aircraft, mainly for older children.

http://inventors.about.com/library/inventors/blhowajetengineworks.htm
How different kinds of jet engines work.

http://www.guncopter.com
All about military helicopters.

http://www.planepictures.net/
Plenty of pictures of all kinds of planes.

Further reading

Planes and Helicopters (Young Machines) by Clive Gifford, Usborne 2004

Aeroplanes (Inside Out) by Chris Oxlade, Franklin Watts 2007

Planes (Extreme Machines) by David Jefferis, Franklin Watts 2009

Tales of Invention: The Aeroplane by Richard & Louise Spilsbury, Heinemann 2010

Now That's Fast: Aircraft by Kate Riggs, Franklin Watts 2011

Note to parents and teachers:

Every effort has been made by the Publishers to ensure that the websites in this book are suitable for children, that they are of the highest educational value, and that they contain no inappropriate or offensive material. However, because of the nature of the Internet, it is impossible to guarantee that the contents of these sites will not be altered. We strongly advise that Internet access is supervised by a responsible adult.

Index